South Africa

The Republic of South Africa occupies the southernmost part of Africa. It covers over 1 million square kilometers (400,000 square miles) of some of the continent's most beautiful land. From the fertile Cape Peninsula to the rugged Drankensberg mountains, and from the veld of the Transvaal to the Natal coast, South Africa abounds with superb scenery. It is famous for its wildlife and game reserves.

South Africans are a unique people, who come from a wide variety of races and cultures. Dutch, English, Africans, and Asians have been brought together, not always peacefully, in a land originally inhabited by Bushmen and nomads.

Vast mineral reserves have meant that South Africa's development into one of the world's leading industrial nations has been rapid, but farming still plays an important part in the economy.

In *We live in South Africa*, a cross-section of the people, men and women, black, white, and "colored" (of mixed descent) describe what life is like in their country – life inland and life on the coast, life in the mines and life on the farms.

Preben Kristensen is a widely traveled photographer and Fiona Cameron is a freelance writer.

ZIMBABWE

BOTSWANA

SOUTH WEST
AFRICA

Kalahari Desert

VENDA

• Pietersburg

Transvaal

BOPHUTHATSWANA

• Sun City

Mala Mala

• Pretoria
• Johannesburg

Randfontein •

SWAZI
LAND

KWAZULU

Orange Free
State

Kimberley •

• Bethlehem

Natal

Buffalo

• Koffiefontein

LESOTHO

Valley of a
Thousand Hill

• Durban

Oranje

TRANSKEI

• De Aar

Cape Province

CISKEI

• Outdshoorn

Cape Town •
Cape Peninsula

• Stellenbosch
Elgin Valley

INDIAN OCEAN

MOZAMBIQUE

we live in
SOUTH AFRICA

Preben Kristensen
and Fiona Cameron

The Bookwright Press
New York · 1985

6-7-95

Living Here

We live in Argentina
We live in Australia
We live in Brazil
We live in Britain
We live in Canada
We live in the Caribbean
We live in Chile
We live in China
We live in Denmark
We live in East Germany
We live in France
We live in Greece
We live in Hong Kong
We live in India
We live in Indonesia
We live in Israel

We live in Italy
We live in Japan
We live in Kenya
We live in Malaysia and Singapore
We live in Mexico
We live in the Netherlands
We live in New Zealand
We live in Pakistan
We live in the Philippines
We live in Poland
We live in South Africa
We live in Spain
We live in Sweden
We live in the Asian U.S.S.R.
We live in the European U.S.S.R.
We live in West Germany

DT 761 K75 1985

The author and publishers would like to acknowledge with thanks the kind help of South African Airways who provided the author with free transport around South Africa.

First published in the United States in 1985 by
The Bookwright Press
387 Park Avenue South
New York, NY 10016

First published in 1985 by
Wayland (Publishers) Ltd
49 Lansdowne Place, Hove
East Sussex BN3 1HF, England

ISBN 0–531–18005–0
Library of Congress Catalog Card Number: 84–73586

Printed by G. Canale & C.S.p.A., Turin, Italy

Contents

"We have to cull 1,500 impala a year"

David Rattray, 26, is a game ranger and manager at Mala Mala, a large private game reserve bordering on the Kruger National Park. He studied zoology and botany at college and came to Mala Mala in 1983.

I spent all my vacations as a child in the bush near the Buffalo River in northern Natal, and practically grew up among the Zulus. They are such magnificent and dignified people. After I left school, I did my national service in South West Africa. My commanding officer used to take me hunting and fishing along the Skeleton Coast. It was really exciting.

I then had five years at college, but even then I used to go off to Botswana or South West Africa in an old jeep for two months every summer.

I started here as a ranger in January 1983 and have been manager since June 1984. It's a great job, especially as we have over 200 different species of animals here, including lion, zebra, cheetah, elephant, hippo, rhino, giraffe, and buffalo. People used to come to hunt game but nowadays the only shooting they're allowed to do is with a camera.

A game ranger has to be a jack-of-all-trades. He has to be able to put up a fence, fix a car engine, and lay a road as well as carry out a whole range of conservation jobs. We try to not interfere with the course of nature here, but when you put a fence around a piece of land like this,

Landrovers are essential for driving over the rough ground at Mala Mala.

animals can't migrate and one species may become strong at the expense of others. We have to cull 1,500 impala a year to keep the balance. It gets rather gory and so we prefer to do it at night under spotlights, but it has to be done.

I don't fear the animals here so much as respect them. People might say that some animals are aggressive and savage but that's because they don't really understand them. Different animals have different needs regarding their territory and may not like you trespassing. You must respect that.

David feels privileged to be so close to wild animals in their natural habitat.

I've had experiences here that I could never have had anywhere else. You see something new every day. For example, I've seen my favorite lioness, "Yellow-tags," give birth in the bush and I've watched a baby leopard, rejected by its mother, trying to survive on its own. I've seen a 35-kilo (75-pound) leopard kill and drag a 70-kilo (150-pound) impala up a tree.

There was a very bad drought here in 1983, and huge numbers of animals were wiped out. You could see them struggling between life and death every day. I find this process fascinating. You can't stop it, it's inevitable. When I see a buffalo being killed by a lion, I don't feel sorry for it. I feel happy because it means that the lion will live for another day.

"I will cost my husband fifteen cows"

Moto Ndlovu, 26, is a Zulu dancer in the Valley of a Thousand Hills in Natal. She has two children, but she cannot marry her boyfriend until he has paid her father. She lives in a *kraal*, a small group of huts, with her family.

I was called Moto because I was born in a motor car, which is quite unusual! My father does woodwork, making bowls and

cooking utensils. He also has sixty head of cattle, so he is wealthy and has been able to afford three wives and sixteen children. We all live together in a *kraal*, which is a group of round, thatched houses. Zulus don't live in square houses because they think there might be evil spirits in the corners. All my father's wives get on well together, but each one has her own separate house. The wives have different ranks in the *kraal*; my mother is the top wife. If one wife died, the others would look after her children. There is plenty of love for everyone.

I started dancing almost as soon as I could stand up. Even though we now dance for tourists, dancing has always been a central part of Zulu culture and there is a special dance for every occasion. There's a dance for welcoming a witch doctor and a special maidens' dance to entertain young men from another *kraal*.

Moto, in Zulu costume, outside one of the huts in the kraal.

We entertain ourselves in the evenings by singing, dancing, and beating the drums. Only unmarried girls can be dancers; once a girl is married she will beat the drums. The young men also dance. They dress up as warriors and for people who don't understand our ceremonies, it can be quite frightening! Girls usually get married at 16, but not many men can afford to marry young. That's because a man has to pay a *lobola* (or bride-price) to the bride's father before he can take her away. The price can be negotiated, but I will cost my husband fifteen cows.

I am 26, but my boyfriend, who is a laborer, has not yet finished paying the *lobola* for me. I have two of his children, who are 5 years and 11 months old, but until he has given my father the last cow of the *lobola* we cannot get married and we must live apart.

Most Zulus can't write, so lovers send love tokens to each other. These are necklaces made out of colored beads.

Men, as well as women, wear special ceremonial clothes for dancing.

Each color means something different, so white means purity and true love, red means intense love, black means anger, and there are many others. You might send your lover a black one if you felt that he was wasting his money and not paying the *lobola* quickly enough!

When we finally get married, I will then go and live with my husband's family. If he were to die, I would then belong to the next brother down in his family.

We always have a big feast at weddings. The drums are beaten, a calf is killed and the bride is given a special goatskin skirt, called a *sidaba*, which she must always wear when she goes out, to show that she is married. One of the worst things that a woman can do is to be found with another man. If she is, she will be sent back to her father, who must return the *lobola* to her husband. It's a terrible disgrace.

9

"An ostrich can kill with a single kick"

Alex Hooper comes from English stock and now owns one of the biggest ostrich farms in South Africa. His family have been involved in ostrich farming at Highgate, near Oudtshoorn, for five generations, but Alex is now using new farming and marketing techniques.

Ostrich feathers have been sought after since the time of the Egyptian pharaohs. A fabulous fan was found in the tomb of Tutankhamun, for the feather in those days was considered a symbol of justice, because it formed equal parts on either side of the quill. At the beginning of this century, the white male feathers were South Africa's fourth largest export after gold, diamonds, and wool. Money poured into the coffers of the feather barons, most of whom squandered their fortunes on "feather palaces" and extravagant living. When the market collapsed at the beginning of World War I, most of them went

These young ostriches are quite tame and it is safe for Alex to walk among them.

bust and about 700,000 of the estimated 750,000 ostriches in existence died of starvation when they were set free to roam in the desert.

However, my family came from a banking background and they were more cautious. We managed to keep the farm going through the bad times and now the business is expanding again. The difference these days is that we use every part of the ostrich, including the meat, the leather, and the eggs, as well as all the feathers. About 120,000 of the 150,000 ostriches currently farmed in South Africa are in Oudtshoorn.

Ostriches are fascinating and unique creatures. They were originally found in desert areas to the north where their feathers, adapted to keep them cool during the day and warm at night, allowed them to survive. Farmers select birds for breeding by the quality of their feathers. Once paired the birds usually stay together for life and they take turns incubating the eggs. The speckled grey female tends them during the day and the black male takes over at night, providing perfect camouflage at all times.

Because ostriches are mute, they have developed elaborate mating and war dances which are very expressive. They are also both fast and dangerous, and an ostrich can kill a man with a single kick. The only thing they seem to respect is a branch of an acacia thorn bush!

In the past, many people used to think that ostriches were killed for their feathers. Gradually, visitors have come to the farms and they have realized that this is not the case. The feathers are merely plucked once every nine months and then regrow naturally. This was the first farm to be opened to the public and now it is a major tourist attraction. Last year we had about 80,000 visitors.

We show visitors the incubators and tell them about the history and habits of the birds. They see how the ostriches are plucked and how the feathers are sorted, and there is even an ostrich race. We also have a restaurant where visitors can taste ostrich steak and eggs. One ostrich egg will make an omelette big enough for twenty-two people.

Ostrich eggs take six weeks to hatch. During this time they are tended by both parents.

"I have seen the sea turn red with blood"

Now 51, Dominic Daniels has been a line fisherman for thirty years and he is the skipper of his brother-in-law's boat. He is married, has six children and eight grandchildren, and lives in a fisherman's flat in Kalk Bay, on the south side of the Cape Peninsula.

Kalk Bay is one of the oldest fishing villages in Cape Province. Both my father and grandfather were fishermen and they taught me all I know. In their day, you used to be able to do some trawling and catch a few crayfish for your family, but nowadays you need a specific license for everything. I've only got a license for line fishing. There used to be hundreds of line fishermen here, but now there are only about fifty of us. Most of the fish are now caught by trawlers. They sweep the banks where the fish breed, so the fish are gradually dying out because they are not given a chance to reproduce.

I go out every day at about 3 a.m. so that we are ready to start fishing at dawn. Sometimes we go farther out and stay away overnight. In fact, we go wherever the fish are. My brother-in-law owns the boat, which is called the *Gwendoline*, but I'm the skipper and I choose the twelve crew members. Each man has his own compartment in the boat, where he keeps his tackle. The boat's owner gets forty percent of any fish caught and the fishermen keep the rest. We catch snoek and hottentot, yellowtails, pangas and, if we go far enough out to sea, tunny.

When the fish are scarce, it's difficult

Up to fifteen men can fish from Dominic's boat.

to get crew. Since they have to pay for their own bait and tackle, it's not worth their while to go out. They get terrible illnesses and stay at home, but as soon as the snoek are back, they're all miraculously cured and want to go out fishing. Today we only caught ten snoek, but on a good day you can catch a hundred. Of course, when you have a good day, so does everyone else, so you have to be the first boat back in order to sell your fish before the price drops. You just can't win!

Snoek, or as it is sometimes known, sea pike, is like mackerel and you can do a lot with it: dry it, fry it, smoke it, or pickle it. The trouble is that the seals like it too. There are hundreds of seals around the Cape, all after the same fish we want. They took more than twenty fish off my line today. We also get trouble from sharks. They fight for the fish on the lines and I

The fish are displayed on the quayside when the boat returns to Kalk Bay.

have seen the sea turn red with blood. If bathers saw what we see out there, I don't think they would ever go swimming along this stretch of coast again.

There are also whales in this area, but they don't trouble us, although they are often bigger than the boat, which is eleven meters (36 feet) long. We were once given an escort by two whales, one on either side of the boat. When we went fast, they went fast, when we slowed down, so did they. They were just playing.

I've never had a vacation. When I can't fish because of the weather, there's always something to do. I make my own tackle and mend it in my spare time. Every fisherman is good at looking after his tackle because he knows that every extra expense will cut down his profit.

Kalk Bay fishermen are still respected everywhere, but I told my sons not to go into fishing because the competition is too tough and you can't make a decent living from it anymore.

"I work at least twelve hours a day"

Corinne Harrison, 28, has been in the hotel industry for ten years. She is now responsible for public relations at a luxury hotel on the outskirts of Johannesburg. She is married, but her career has meant she hasn't had time for any children yet.

I was born in Germiston, near Johannesburg. I went to school there, but left at 16 to go to a hotel training college in Johannesburg for a year to train as a receptionist. I visited a number of different hotels during the course, but when I walked through the doors of the Landrost, I knew that it was the one for me. I started work there when I was 17, on January 1, 1975, and stayed there for eight years. The hotel was a nice size, with 265 rooms and about 300 employees. I did everything from reception to housekeeping and finally made it to the number three position as the manager of the Rooms Division in 1978.

In January 1983, I was given the chance to work on the development of a new hotel with my former boss. He treats me as if I were a man and calls me Harry, but we work well together. We had to make decisions about everything, from uniform design to the pattern of the cutlery and crockery; from menus to the choice of mints. It was a real hotbed of activity. Finally, we got the management team

together and the Sandton Sun Hotel opened on January 27, 1984, my fifth wedding anniversary.

I think that every hotelier must be good at public relations. My duties here are to ensure the guests are properly looked after. I check the lists of arrivals, make

The enormous lobby of the Sandton Sun Hotel.

Corinne has reached a senior position in the hotel industry at the age of 28.

sure that queries and complaints are dealt with, meet and entertain VIPs, and keep in contact with long-term guests. This is primarily a businessman's hotel, so punctual wake-up calls, flight information, and general efficiency are vital.

I work at least twelve hours a day, six days a week. My husband used to be in the hotel trade, so he understands my way of life. Anyway, it means that he can go off and play golf for hours on end while I'm working. Both he and my colleagues accept my success in the business world and it is not as unusual as it used to be for a woman to reach my level.

It's a hectic, stressful life, but I'm a calm person. I've learned to look at the warning signals both in my marriage and in my work. I try to act on those signals, usually by taking a weekend off and getting completely away from the hotel business. I'm ambitious and I love my work, but I do try to keep what little private life I have completely private.

I'd like to have children and bring them up in a hotel environment, but I'm not ready for it yet. Being a hotelier is a way of life, not just a job. Perhaps one day, if we ever get a little country hotel of our own, it will be possible. But that's something for the future.

"Our gold is worth 8 billion rand a year"

Wilberforce Ndamase is a 34-year-old gold miner at Randfontein Gold Mines on the Witwatersrand gold reef outside Johannesburg. He lives in a hostel near the mine, but his wife and children live hundreds of miles away in the Transkei.

I've been a gold miner at Randfontein for twelve years. I've had various jobs in the mines since I began as a winch driver. I then became a train driver and, in 1975, I was trained to be a team leader. The job involved five weeks of special training, in which I learned simple arithmetic and how to take precise measurements.

I now have a crew of thirty-eight, including two gang supervisors. One supervisor is responsible for the mine's timber supports, the other for moving the ore away from the face. The men come from Lesotho, Swaziland, Mozambique, Zululand, and the Transkei, but we don't have any language problems as everyone speaks Fanakalo.

We work the morning shift, from 6 a.m. until 2 p.m., five days a week. The mines can be up to 3 kilometers (2 miles) deep, and underground there is a huge network of tunnels. The deepest mine shaft in the world is at the Western Deep Levels Mine: it is 3,859 meters (12,660 feet) below the surface. Each mine has hundreds of miles of railway for transporting the ore. There is always water in the tunnels and it's extremely hot and humid. It's also very noisy because of the drills and explosives.

We get only about 10 grams of gold for

Wilberforce teaches a new miner how to build roof supports.

As team leader, Wilberforce must be sure that the equipment is safe before mining begins.

every ton of rock that we excavate, which is one of the reasons why gold is so expensive. Even so, we produce 120 kilos of gold at this mine every week, and South Africa produces over 600 tons of gold every year, which is fifty-five percent of all the gold mined in the world. Our gold is worth 8 billion rand ($4 billion) a year. The major currencies of the world would collapse without South African gold.

My father is a chieftain and head of the *kraal*, or family group. Most of the young men in the *kraal* live and work away from home and send their wages back to their families. My older brother works in Rustenburg 130 kilometers away, but when my father dies, he will have to go home and take over as chieftain.

I live in a hostel here at the mine with eleven others, all from the Transkei. I go home twice a month to see my wife and three children. The bus leaves here on Friday night and comes back on Sunday night. It takes all night just to get there. You can only get a contract to work for about nine months at one stretch and then you must go home for at least three months. I don't work when I'm home with my family. I would like to have my family with me all the time, but my home is in the Transkei and my job is in Randfontein.

"We produce 10,000 tons of apples a year"

Jimmy Rawbone-Viljoen is 64 and owns the Oak Valley Estate, which is one of the biggest apple farms in Elgin Valley, in Cape Province. His family has been growing apples for eighty years, and the farm now employs over 200 people.

My grandfather bought this farm in 1899 and planted the first apple tree in this valley in 1903. Now Elgin Valley and Vyeboom Valley, which is next to it, produce about sixty-four percent of all African apples grown south of the Sahara Desert.

During the winter the trees are pruned, so they can bear more fruit.

That's largely because of the favorable climate in this area. We have fairly cool winters, with temperatures dropping below 10°C (50°F), fairly hot summers averaging 30°C (86°F) by day, and we get between 70 and 90 centimeters (27 to 35 inches) of rain a year. Most important, we're free from hail here. In fact, you could probably grow apples all across the

country if it weren't for the hail.

I've been running the farm since the end of World War II, and I've seen several developments in the industry since then. During the war, South Africa was prevented from exporting fruit overseas, so most of our fruit was canned. When peace was restored, our packaging equipment had become obsolete, so some of us got together in 1948 to form a cooperative which would deal with both packaging and marketing, in order to cut costs.

Before the war, much of the land had been left undeveloped because irrigation was difficult on the undulating terrain of the region. So, between 1948 and 1950, we started the first piped irrigation projects. As a result of that, production was pushed up from about 25 tons per hectare (10 tons per acre) to between 50 and 100 tons per hectare. On average, we produce about 10,000 tonnes of apples a year on this farm.

More recently, we have followed the Americans in using chemicals. Some are used to protect the fruit from disease, while others regulate the size and quality. We have also been using Controlled Atmosphere Cold Storage facilities for about the last seven years, which means that we can keep apples for up to nine months, instead of only three.

Of course, all these factors mean higher production but there is also much greater competition, especially as a result of growing protectionism in the EEC (European Economic Community). My grandfather experimented with fifty different varieties of apple, but now we grow only Granny Smiths, Golden Delicious, and a few types of Red Delicious. Our aim is to produce only top quality fruit and any that is not quite up to standard is used to make apple juice. Last year I exported about 16,000

Jimmy's farm is one of the biggest in the fertile Elgin Valley.

boxes of Granny Smiths.

One thing that hasn't really changed is the fact that it's a very labor intensive business, although more sophisticated skills are required now that we're spending up to 200,000 rand ($100,000) a year on spraying materials alone. We have about 140 permanent staff, whom we house on the farm, and an extra 100 workers are employed during the harvest season. But throughout the year, there's always a lot to do. The trees are constantly being pruned during the winter. In November, the peaches and apricots need harvesting and then the apples ripen at different rates until finally the Granny Smiths are ready for harvesting at the beginning of May, which is the autumn in South Africa. The apple trees have to be sprayed sixteen or seventeen times during the summer before the harvest.

"When I'm not doing housework I'm studying"

Sarah Nonkanyiso, 17, lives in the black township of Umlazi, 8 kilometers south of Durban. She is in the "Standard 8" class at the local secondary school, but she has to spend a lot of her time looking after her family. Sarah wants to become a teacher.

I get up at six o'clock every day, do housework, and prepare breakfast for my family. I live with my grandmother, my mother, my sister, her two children, and my brother, who is an industrial worker. At 7:30 a.m. I walk to school, which is in Section V of the township, about thirty minutes away.

My mother is 42 and she works as a cleaning lady. She pays for my school fees, uniform, exam fees, and books. It is hard to afford on her pay, but we think education is very important. My sister works as a seamstress and earns thirty-two rand a week. Her husband is no good – he left her on her own with the children, who are now looked after by my grandmother.

Our school day normally has two breaks: fifteen minutes in the morning and thirty minutes for lunch. In the lunch break we buy bread and soup from a store nearby. We finish school at 3:30 p.m. Thursday is our day for sports: the girls play basketball and the boys play soccer. There are 653 pupils in the school and ten classrooms. I love English, but I also find mathematics, biology, and geography very interesting subjects.

When I get home from school, I have to clean the house, which has four rooms, prepare the family's dinner, and do the

There are more than fifty pupils in Sarah's class.

Sarah likes her school, but education is expensive for black children's families.

dishes. Often it's nine o'clock before I can start my homework, so during the week, when I'm not doing housework, I'm studying. I don't get much sleep. On weekends, I either go out with my friends or do the family's washing. I have a very close friend called Sophie, who is 18. We often study together in the evenings.

The school system in South Africa consists of ten "Standards": 1, 2, 3, etcetera up to Standard 10. Lower primary school is Substandards A and B (nursery school) and Standards 1 and 2. Higher primary school is Standards 3, 4, 5 and 6. At this stage you have to take an exam, known as Form One. You then go on to secondary school, which is Standards 7 and 8, and finally high school, which is Standards 9 and 10. When I have finished Standard 10 I hope to be accepted at Pietermaritzburg Teacher's College for a three-year teacher training course.

My boyfriend, who is 19, is at high school in Standard 9. We don't have much time to spend with each other and it will take some time before we can get married. To marry me, he will have to pay between ten and fifteen cows, maybe even more because I'll have had a good education. Educated women are worth a lot more than uneducated ones.

"Some people call it 'Sin City'"

Marc Roussos, 35, used to be a dealer on the Johannesburg Stock Exchange. Then, after eight years as a caterer, he came to work at Sun City, a huge hotel and entertainment complex in the independent state of Bophuthatswana.

Sun City is built in an old volcanic crater, set in the Pilansberg mountains. It was officially opened by the President of Bophuthatswana, Lucas Mangope, in December 1979. More than 1.5 million visitors now come here every year because

Formerly a barren crater, Sun City is now one of Africa's most luxurious resorts.

Sun City provides something for everyone. There is a sports arena, casino, slot machines, waterworld, golf course, tennis courts, BMX track, health center, conference facilities, and every kind of restaurant imaginable.

The Republic of Bophuthatswana is an independent state, although the United Nations refuses to recognize it, saying it is controlled by South Africa. The government here believes in free enterprise and there is no apartheid. Sun City is a racial experiment and it is proving successful. Although 95 percent of the guests staying overnight in the hotel are white, over 60 percent of the day visitors are black. Ninety percent of our visitors come from South Africa or the other independent black states and they come by plane, bus, and car. They may spend 50 cents or 1,000 rand ($500); they may stay for a few hours or as long as a month.

Some people call it "Sin City" because of the gambling, which is forbidden in South Africa. These people forget, though, how important Sun City is for the economy and future development of Bophuthatswana. Along with about 500 Whites, Sun City now employs more than 1,900 members of the local Tswana tribe – a number which is constantly growing. A lot of these employees have no previous experience in this kind of work, so we provide on-the-job training. We also create a lot of indirect employment for people in related industries.

Since the Bophuthatswana Development Corporation has a stake in Sun City, we work closely with the government in the planning and development of services in the surrounding villages. We have already financed 350 apartments and 250 houses for the staff, and more are planned.

Sun City's main attraction: row upon row of "one-armed bandits."

Sun City also provides a bus service to the schools in Rustenberg, 30 kilometers (20 miles) away, and gives financial support to a school for the deaf and dumb.

My father was Greek and my mother English, but I was born in South Africa. After school, I became a dealer on the Johannesburg Stock Exchange, which I left soon after the crash of 1968 and went into the catering business for about eight years. I catered weddings, cocktail parties, conferences, and large trade fairs. I had decided to sell my business and go to the United States when I came to Sun City on vacation in 1981. I've been here ever since, first in charge of the Food and Beverage Department and then from 1982, as a resident manager. I'm currently working on two new restaurants in a spectacular new hotel being built here, which is a very exciting challenge.

"We are not paid to get hurt"

At 30, Vernon Hunter is already a lieutenant in the South African Police Force and is in charge of a police station in Umbilo, a white residential suburb of Durban. He came to Durban from Johannesburg, to be near his wife's family.

I was brought up in Koffiefontein in the Orange Free State. When I finished school at 18, I applied to join the police. I went to Police Training College in Pretoria for a year's basic training. They give you infantry drill and teach you to use firearms effectively. They also teach you counter-insurgency techniques. A police training exempts you from military service, although you may be called up to do border duty from time to time.

After basic training, I was posted to the Flying Squad in Johannesburg for five years. That's the branch that deals with all the serious crimes. Of course, some of the crimes are so shocking that they leave a deep impression on you, but it was also very interesting work.

In 1976, I asked for an exchange transfer to Durban. At the moment I'm in command of Umbilo police station, which has 110 uniformed policemen and about 30 detectives. Umbilo is about 18 square kilometers (7 square miles) in size, with about 100,000 inhabitants. I live with my family in a subsidized police house next to the police station.

The police headquarters are in Pretoria. The country is divided into 19 divisions, comprising 84 police districts, 843 police

Vernon is issued special equipment for his work with the Durban Anti-Riot Unit.

24

Durban faces many of the vice problems found in most large cities.

stations and 39 border control posts. The Port Natal division contains five districts and is the largest in the country.

The force is open to all races and contains a substantial number of women. Everyone has the same opportunities. In June 1981, there were 62 police stations manned exclusively by non-white members; 47 manned by Blacks, 14 by Coloreds and 1 by Indians. Durban is a multiracial city, so it's important that all groups should be represented. We have about fifty percent white and fifty percent non-white policemen here.

I am also in charge of the Durban Anti-Riot Unit. Our job in the Anti-Riot Unit is to prevent people getting injured, and the training bears this in mind. We have to be able to protect ourselves as well, as we are not paid to get hurt.

Durban is reasonably safe, but it's a big port, so the harbor tends to attract vices such as drugs, prostitution and, consequently, some violence. Fortunately, we do not have a problem with hard drugs in this country. The most common crimes are burglaries, car thefts, stock thefts, robberies and assaults. There are about 40,000 policemen altogether in the country, and the number is fixed by the government.

"Mrs Ples is about 3 million years old"

Robert Burrett is 20 years old and is a third year student of archaeology and human geography at the Witwatersrand University in Johannesburg. He has worked on several digs and he hopes to become a lecturer in archaeology.

"Wits" is one of the biggest and best universities in South Africa and it's therefore very difficult to get in. You have to go all the way to "Standard Ten" at school and then take the South African university entrance exam. There are about 15,000 students here altogether. Most are white, but since 1971, Blacks, Coloreds, Chinese, and Indians have also been accepted, although they have to get a government permit first. It's difficult to get a permit and there are only about 2,000 non-white students here at the moment but it is to be hoped that the number will increase.

University tuition is expensive in this country. I live at home and my parents support me and pay my fees. The few undergraduate grants available go to "practical" departments like geology, engineering, and computing. Archaeology is considered a luxury, but if I get into a postgraduate course, I should get a grant to cover my fees. In my subject, the only way to get funds for research work is to be a lecturer or work in a museum. I would

The quarry at Sterkfontein is one of Africa's most important archaeological sites.

Robert holds a copy of Sterkfontein no.5, otherwise known as Mrs. Ples.

like to be a lecturer here at "Wits."

I find archaeology so exciting that it takes up all my time. I went on my first dig at the age of 12 and I've always been fascinated by man's past. I go to digs whenever I can. We work as a team, excavating sites slowly and carefully, so we don't destroy any valuable artifacts. Excavation work is mentally as well as physically demanding because you have to be both patient and alert. I've been lucky because there are very good teachers here and one of the most important sites in South Africa is an old lime quarry at Sterkfontein, only forty kilometers northwest of Johannesburg. It was here, on April 18, 1947, that a fossilized skull was discovered by Dr Robert Broom and his assistant John Robinson.

It was given the name *Plesianthropus transvaalensis*, but because it was a female skull it soon came to be known as "Mrs. Ples." Not only did Mrs. Ples provide a missing link between the ape-man and the hominid, both ancestors of modern man, but she also had one of the best preserved prehistoric skulls ever found.

Mrs. Ples would have looked quite like us except for her facial features. She stood erect and walked on two feet, although she would have been quite small, about 1.37 meters (4½ feet) tall. We think that Mrs. Ples is about 3 million years old, although dating a discovery like this is very difficult. It can only be done by studying the tools, flora, and fauna discovered in a dig, and by comparing them with other dated discoveries. When you think that *homo sapiens* is only 70,000 years old, a discovery like this really puts mankind in perspective.

"The basic problem is poverty"

Sybil Hotz has been a councilor on the Durban City Council since 1974 and was deputy mayor and then mayor between 1978 and 1984. Durban is the most culturally diverse city in the country, which causes problems but also presents new opportunities.

Our city is administered by the Durban Metropolitan Council. The white inhabitants elect thirty councilors, who in turn elect the mayor and deputy mayor.

Among other things, the council is responsible for the supply of water and electricity, roads, housing, town planning, transportation, sanitation, and health services. Ours, however, is not just a council for Whites. All races in South Africa are going to share the future together and there is no way you can hold back the process of change. Our society is changing and I think that, with good planning and bold decisions, Durban will become an open, multiracial city.

It was a great honor and responsibility for me to be Mayor of Durban for four years. The University of Durban gave me an honorary doctorate for my contributions to the welfare of our city's ethnic groups. I've always felt that the mayor belongs to all the people, both the voters and the voteless.

During the last two years of my term, I organized an annual breakfast for 900 children representing every ethnic group in Durban, to give them a chance to meet, talk, and make friends. Other attempts at

Sybil Hotz has enjoyed both the prestige and the pressure of public office.

communication between races have arisen as a result of those breakfasts, and I believe that it is an important start on the road to racial integration.

I was trained as a nurse and I married a general practitioner, so I've always been involved in listening to and dealing with other people's problems. Even so, the public duties expected of a mayor were very demanding. In my last year in the job, I was invited to more than 1,200 functions. I went to as many as possible and enjoyed them all, from the grandest banquet to the smallest backyard event. I am still interested in the running of the city and you don't need a mayoral chain

A city of contrasts: behind the impressive Durban seafront lie areas of great poverty.

around your neck to be active, aware, and involved in public service.

I chaired the Durban Housing Committee for three years and I have studied housing in the United States, Hong Kong, Singapore, and South America. People say that to cure poor living conditions we should build more houses, but that doesn't solve the basic problem, which is poverty. If you can cure the poverty, then there won't be a housing problem.

In local government, people are more interested in what you do for them than your political ideologies. There are practical methods that can be used to improve the living standards of all South Africans, and here in Durban we're in a position to show the country what can be achieved through change.

"Bargaining is part of the fun"

A. M. Patel is the owner of three stores in the Oriental Plaza, a big shopping center in Johannesburg where only Asians are allowed to trade. He is fifty-nine and has been involved in retailing since his father died forty-four years ago. He is married and has three children.

Asians and retailing have become almost synonymous in South Africa. Athough the first Indians who came to South Africa in 1860 were brought over to be laborers on the Natal sugar plantations, large numbers also came into the country as traders, merchants, and craftsmen.

I was born into a family of traders. My grandfather was a peddler. He traveled around the country selling everything from buttons to crockery, so trading is very

The shops in the plaza cater to all races, although only Asians can own them.

much in my family's blood.

The first store I owned was a ladies' underwear boutique, then I had a glass and china shop, and then a store which sold curtain material. I did well with all of them. When the Asians were told to move their premises from Diagonal Street to the new Oriental Plaza, we were not pleased with the idea. For several decades we'd been trading from small stores, displaying most of our wares on the narrow pavements outside.

Today Diagonal Street is the site of the Johannesburg Stock Exchange. The picturesque little stores have all disappeared and we now trade in this modern shopping plaza. Visitors come from far and wide to buy anything from jewelry to a real Indian curry. Everybody knows that you never pay the price marked on the product and bargaining is part of the fun of shopping here.

Most of the stores here operate on a low profit margin and high turnover. Renting the store is not cheap: I pay 210 rand ($105) a month for my 16 square meters (172 sq ft) of floor space. I do well enough though. I own a comfortable house in Lenasia, the Indian township outside Johannesburg, and I hope to retire soon.

The government did once provide a voluntary repatriation plan for Indians, whereby they were each given a free passage and a cash bonus to return to India. However, very few Indians made use of this offer and today we are accepted as part of the South African community. We are moving beyond our traditional roles and nowadays you will find many Indians who are prosperous merchants, brokers, lawyers, doctors, building contractors, industrialists, and manufacturers.

We have maintained our Indian culture, but at the same time, we are still very

The Oriental Plaza was designed with space and comfort very much in mind.

much a part of South Africa. In Durban, which has the largest Indian community in South Africa, we have our own university, the University of Durban-Westville. Most of us speak English and some speak a little Afrikaans, but the older generation to which I belong generally speaks Indian languages, such as Tamil, Hindi, Telugu, Gujarati, and Urdu. Most Indians are either Muslims, like myself, or Hindus, but a small group are members of the Dutch Reformed Church.

Indians have just been given the right to vote for their own representatives in the House of Deputies, which is a step forward for us. But there is a long way to go and my children will have to work for further rights if they want them. As for myself, I've established three sound businesses and I now live comfortably and peacefully, as a good Muslim should.

"All told, I speak nine languages"

Alex Simelane is 51 and has worked in the mining industry since 1959. He lives in subsidized married quarters with his wife and three daughters at the Randfontein Gold Mine, where he is an aptitude tester and a teacher of Fanakalo, a language used in the mines.

I am a Zulu, but I was born in the married quarters here at Randfontein. I've been working in the staff training section of the mines since 1959 and live in subsidized married quarters, with my wife and three daughters. There are eighty-four of us

Alex's house is owned and subsidized by the mining company.

altogether in the staff training center. I have two jobs here. One is as an aptitude tester and the other is as a teacher of Fanakalo, a special language developed for use in the mines.

A very wide range of people come to work here, both from within South Africa and from neighboring countries, and they all have their own languages, cultural

backgrounds, and levels of education and training. So, on arrival, newcomers go through a number of examinations to measure their physical fitness and general aptitude for learning new skills. The end results are passed on to the "labor distributor" and the employee will then be given a job to suit his capabilities. My job as an aptitude tester is, then, a very responsible one, and I enjoy it very much.

Of course, employing people from so many different areas results in huge language problems as most employees speak neither English nor Afrikaans, the official South African languages. Each region of this country has its own language or dialect, which can't always be understood by people of another region. For example, there are eight officially recognized black, or Bantu, languages in South Africa. The official ones are Zulu, Xhosa, Swazi, Northern, Western, and Southern Sotho, Venda, and Tsonga. Some of these languages are closely related, but others differ greatly. In addition, there are several languages spoken which are not recognized by the government, and each one has many different dialects.

There are also the Hottentot and Bushman languages. The Hottentots and Bushmen are the non-Negro tribes who originally inhabited most of southern Africa, before they became absorbed by black tribes migrating southward. But some Hottentot tribes are still to be found in South West Africa, and Bushmen in the Kalahari Desert. Their languages are unlike any others in the world, although the clicking sounds they use have become partly absorbed into the Bantu languages. All told, I speak nine languages, including English and Afrikaans, and I am learning others.

Fanakalo has been developed over the last 100 years to overcome the difficulties of communication among mine workers of different origins. Mining can be dangerous if safety measures are not properly carried out, so it is very important for people here to understand each other. Fanakalo is based on Zulu, although it includes modified English and Afrikaans words such as *hamela*, from "hammer" and *bokis*, from "box."

There are only three Fanakalo teachers here. Although there are about 13,000 employees at the mine, there are very few novices these days. I have taught about 100 this year. A Zulu or Xhosa will learn Fanakalo in under four days whereas a white person might take two weeks. After that, it doesn't matter how many different tribal groups work together, they can all speak a common language.

New miners spend as much as two weeks in Alex's classroom before going underground.

"Trust is so important in this business"

Johannes Swart was born in Bethlehem in the Orange Free State on Christmas Day, 1934. He has been a dealer in rough diamonds since 1981, and he is also a staff officer in command of an army unit in Johannesburg.

I've been in several different businesses but I've always been fascinated by the diamond industry. I got into it through contacts in the army, which also plays an important part in my life. It teaches you self-discipline and it builds up your resistance to hardship. That's a good training for this business!

Diamonds are the hardest substance known to man, and they are therefore valuable industrially as well as for ornament. They occur in a rock called kimberlite, which is found all over South Africa. When they are first mined, all the diamonds are rough, but they may be of either gem or industrial quality depending on how suitable they are for cutting. Here in South Africa, we are the world's largest producer of gem diamonds. Kimberley is the center of the industry, but there are diamond mines stretching right across the north of the country.

There are still a few individuals who get their licenses and go out looking for diamonds with a pick, shovel, and sieve, just as they did in the early days of prospecting. Nowadays, however, most diamonds are mined by one of the twenty-seven big producers, most of which are controlled, directly or indirectly, by De Beers Consolidated Mines. In fact, De Beers and its subsidiaries are responsible for most of the world's diamond production.

The producer sells the diamonds either directly to a diamond cutting works or to a rough diamond dealer, who will then sell them to diamond cutting works all over the world.

To deal in rough diamonds, you need a special dealer's license, which can only be issued to an individual and not a company. A deal between a dealer and a producer, worth maybe $5,000,000, is made verbally and without any written contract. As trust is so important in this business, the Diamond and Gold Branch of the police investigates your background, financial circumstances, and knowledge of diamonds very carefully before letting you

diamonds. The more unusual colors are pink, green, or blue. Ten dealers looking at a rough diamond will offer ten different prices. A dealer's skill enables him to see the promise in a rough diamond, but it may turn out to be illusory once he starts cutting it. Dealing in diamonds is a combination of knowledge and luck.

Kimberley Big Hole, a disused diamond mine, has a circumference of nearly 12 kilometers (7½ miles).

Johannes doesn't need much equipment, apart from a safe.

loose with a dealer's license.

Before I applied for my license I spent four months in a cutting factory learning about all aspects of cutting diamonds. That experience has proved invaluable.

There are fewer categories of rough diamonds than polished ones. Basically you get white, off-white, and yellow

"I use my powers only to help people"

Bella Komane, 51, is married and has four children. She is a full-time elementary school teacher, a part-time announcer on Radio Tswana, and a spiritual herbalist. She lives in a black township just outside Pretoria.

I prefer to be called a spiritual herbalist rather than a witch doctor, because witch doctors can both harm and cure, whereas I am a Christian and only use my powers to help people.

I have brought up four children and sent them to college. It's very expensive and I couldn't survive by just curing people. Anyhow, most of the time I do it for nothing. I never ask for money from a patient. To support ourselves, my husband works for Radio Tswana and I teach.

I am Tswana by birth. As early as I can remember, my family consulted me before taking any major decision. I am a Christian and I was afraid of my powers and, for a long time, I fought against developing them. In the end though, if you ignore the spirits of your ancestors, they will make you ill until you accept them and listen to what they say. That's what happened to me until finally, in 1977, I gave in. I spent several months in Pietersburg and Zimbabwe, or Rhodesia as it was then, learning the traditional methods used by witch doctors. I was taught how to collect and use herbs, but many of the witch doctors were quacks and it was difficult to find good doctors. But I got my certificate, which means that I am qualified to administer herbal medicines to people.

Every year I go north to collect herbs. I usually visit the Ndebele tribe of the northern Transvaal, who are the people who moved north from the original Zulu kingdom. They are very knowledgeable about medicine and know where to find all the best herbs. I enjoy staying with them because they are such an interesting tribe. Their art and clothes form a very colorful part of southern African culture, which it is important to preserve.

My people expect me to use traditional rituals, but I don't really need them. Many witch doctors beat drums and make a lot of music, but I don't feel I need to.

However, most people like me to "throw the bones" to divine the patient's problem. The patient blows into the bag of bones and then I throw them onto the floor. I

some emotional problems, the patient must help himself. There are a lot of emotional illnesses these days. Many people seem to be more interested in money than in leading a good life.

I don't seek patients. They hear of me from their friends and come to me for help. I have very little free time, but next year I'll spend all my time helping people.

Two Ndebele women display wares made in the tribe's traditional manner.

Bella points out the meaning of the bones, using a deer's leg.

can tell by the pattern in which they fall what the problem is. There are many different bones and shells including two special "God bones," one for the patient's paternal ancestors and one for his maternal ancestors. Once I have discovered the problem, there are herbs to be given to the patient if his illness is physical. Some of these herbs are very dangerous, so you must use them properly. However, for

"Ultimately I have the last word"

Johannes Wessel Greeff, a 62-year-old lawyer, lives in Cape Town. He became interested in politics at an early age and has been a Member of Parliament since 1973. In 1983, he became Speaker of Parliament and is responsible for keeping order in the chamber.

The processes of government have always interested me. What started as curiosity about politics at a very early age soon became an urge actually to participate in the political field in South Africa.

I'm now the Speaker of Parliament and I'm responsible for the proper maintenance of order in its various chambers. It does happen that I sometimes have to ask someone to withdraw a remark if I consider it to be unparliamentary. If he refuses, I can order him to leave the chamber for the rest of the day. No one in Parliament can go against my rulings because, ultimately, I have the last word.

The new South African constitution was passed in September 1984. The Parliament consists of three chambers: the House of Assembly (made up of 178 Whites), the House of Representatives (made up of eighty-five Coloreds) and the House of Deputies (made up of forty-five Indians). All Whites, Coloreds, and Indians, who are South African citizens over the age of 18, may register as voters for their respective house of Parliament.

Being Speaker is a full-time job and Johannes has little time for hobbies.

Blacks cannot vote for the South African Parliament. Members of Parliament are normally elected for a period of five years.

The President is selected for a similar period by an electoral college of eighty-eight Members of Parliament, drawn from all three houses. He is the chairman of the Cabinet, which consists of an unspecified number of ministers who handle all matters of common or national interest. The Cabinet also includes three councils which attend to matters concerning their own population groups. The Cabinet ministers need not be Members of Parliament, but the representatives on the three councils must be drawn from their own respective houses in Parliament.

There is also a President's Council with sixty members, some of whom are elected and some appointed by the President. This council advises the President on any matter of national importance and acts as an

The Parliament buildings in Cape Town.

arbiter in the event of any conflict among the three houses.

Although Blacks are not represented in Parliament, they have been given self-rule in ten black national states within the borders of South Africa. Four of these states, Transkei, Bophuthatswana, Venda and Ciskei, have been granted the status of independent republics. KwaZulu, Qwaqwa, Lebowa, Gazankulu, KaNgwane and KwaNdebele will eventually be offered independence from South Africa.

Many Blacks, however, live around the major cities in the so-called black townships. The larger townships have their own town councils and are empowered to manage their own affairs. They are comparable to the white town councils. The smaller townships have village councils, with varying degrees of responsibility.

39

"Our wines are among the finest in the world"

Christian Joubert is a wine producer at the Spier estate, near Stellenbosch, in the wine-growing region of Cape Province. His cellar is one of the sixteen which make up the Wine Route, which was set up to encourage people to find out more about South African wines.

Jan van Riebeeck not only established the first settlement at the Cape of Good Hope, he also established the vineyards from which South Africa's first wine was produced in 1659. In its early years the Cape produced heavy, sweet wines. The most famous of these was Constantia, which was to be found in the cellars of Napoleon, Wellington, and Bismarck, among others.

Nowadays there are 6,000 farmers making approximately 600 million liters (850 million bottles) of wine a year. Most of the vineyards are in southwestern Cape Province and I think it is fair to say that our wines now include some of the finest in the world. The gross value of South Africa's annual wine production is about 150 million rand ($75 million). Most of the vines were originally imported from Europe and the types are largely comparable to French and German ones, although we have developed special breeds such as Pinotage. The soil and climate of South Africa are different from those of Europe, and this also affects the taste of the wine. The absence of harsh frosts and the relative consistency of the climate mean that vintages differ less drastically from year

The new leaves start to appear on the vines in early spring.

to year than they do in Europe. However, until fairly recently, the South African market was small and unsophisticated, so little effort was made to produce wines of great quality.

I think that things have changed a great deal over the last few years, especially since the development of the Wine Route, which was officially opened in 1971. This now involves twelve private cellars and five cooperative wineries, all of which are open to the public and encourage people to taste and learn about their wines. Last year we had more than 100,000 visitors.

In 1973, South Africa introduced a system of origin determination. This means that each bottle is classified according to its origin and it keeps poor quality wines from being passed off as good ones. Quality and price controls are maintained by the KWV, a producer organization set up by the wine farmers in 1918 to manage their affairs. The KWV also handles most of South Africa's wine exports, which are growing rapidly. We now export wine to more than twenty-five different countries, although ninety percent of our total production is still consumed in South Africa.

On my farm, I have a restaurant which serves traditional food, but I'm not as interested in commercialization as I am in maintaining quality. However, I have to admit it is a big farming operation, with 400 hectares (990 acres) of land, producing about 5,000 bottles of wine per hectare. There are also 100 employees to keep happy. At the end of the day though, there's nothing as nice as sitting under a tree tasting a glass of your own wine – perhaps a Spier Colombar.

The estate at Spier, which now houses a restaurant as well as an extensive cellar.

"We carry over 4 million people a year"

Danie van Zyl is 29 and he has spent the last eleven years working as an aircraft technician for South African Airways. He lives with his wife and two daughters in Kempton Park, near Jan Smuts airport, Johannesburg.

In 1984, South African Airways celebrated fifty years of successful operation. We have progressed from owning only four single-engine planes in 1934 to today's fleet of fifty modern airliners. We now carry over 4 million people a year.

Danie sits on a Boeing 747's engine. Fully loaded, the plane weighs 365 tons.

In 1934 there was no regular air service between South Africa and London. Occasionally, attempts were made to break existing records for the journey, which then took four or five days. Today, SAA offers an eleven-hour non-stop service from London to Johannesburg. Things haven't always been so easy: on August 22, 1963, a number of black states across the African continent banned SAA planes from their airspace and threatened to shoot down any plane breaking the ban. We were forced to re-route all our European flights overnight, and instead of cutting across Africa, we had to fly the much longer route around the west coast. This, however, prompted us to devise new ways of making the engines more efficient. Eventually, cooperation with the engine manufacturer resulted in an improved version being designed. This new version, in fact, gave us nineteen percent more take-off thrust and saved fuel consumption when cruising.

I started working for SAA after school,

Danie works on a variety of planes. The one in the foreground is a Boeing 737.

at the age of 18. I trained for three years to become an aircraft technician, but that was only the basic training. After that, I had to take various courses on different types of aircraft, such as the Boeing 747, and the Airbus A300. Even if the different airplanes operate on the same principle, it is very important to know all the specific characteristics of the one that you are working on.

My work at SAA was interrupted when I was drafted to do my military service in the Infantry Corps. I'm now a major in the Commandos, which is a special force created to defend our local areas. I have to serve for one month every year to keep up my military skills and, in addition, I spend each Wednesday night doing the necessary administrative work.

Here at Jan Smuts airport there are ninety technicians in all, and we work in three shifts around the clock. Apart from good technical knowledge, you need discipline and a sense of responsibility in order to become a good aircraft technician. We are often sent on short missions to neighboring countries to do maintenance work on our planes there. That's how we became known as The Flying Spanners!

"I was suddenly a person in great demand"

Johannes Mpuri, 47, has been a self-employed architectural draftsman in the Johannesburg area for the last eight years. He did not attend school regularly, but he trained on the job. He is married and has four children.

I got my first job at 18, working in a clothing factory. Then, when I was 23, I started as a print boy at L&F Metter, a structural steel engineering firm. I was there for seventeen years. After six years, I was promoted to driver and eventually became the personal driver for Mr F. Metter himself. He was an excellent man, the man who really set me on my way.

I was an artist in my spare time and someone offered to train me as a draftsman in the drawing office. I hadn't learned much math at school and found it difficult, but Mr Metter forced me to keep trying. It was fourteen months before I really started enjoying life again. After six years, I had become one of their best and highest paid draftsmen.

I started drawing houseplans for friends in the evening and made more money making two plans a week than I was being paid for an entire week's work at L&F Metter. I stopped needing my salary. I got so much work that I had to take a couple of weeks' vacation to try to get through it. I was suddenly a person in great demand. Then I got even more work, so eventually I left and started working for myself. At first my wife was very unhappy that I had given up such a good job but now she's pleased because she doesn't have to work any more. Also now that I work from home, I can choose my own hours and

Johannes drew the plans for his own house and supervised its construction.

Johannes talks to a local bishop in front of the church he designed.

this has given me the chance to travel and see other parts of the country.

I've made thousands and thousands of plans in the last eight years; for houses, stores, and churches all over the place. I use building contractors to do the work itself, but I also supervise them if my client wants me to.

At the moment, I'm doing quite a lot of work in Tokoza and Katlehong, black townships on the outskirts of Johannesburg. The townships are growing quickly as people come to the cities to find work.

I've designed several supermarkets in Tokoza as well as houses and factories. I work more cheaply than an architect and I get so much work that I can hardly cope. In fact, I've had a girl helping me for about a year and now I'm training her.

I've designed a lot of churches but I never charge very much for them. They have to be very special as they are public places. I am a Catholic and go to church every Sunday and sometimes during the week as well, if I can. The Church is a very important part of our lives here.

I have two boys and two girls. I don't choose their careers, but they must do something constructive with their lives.

"Someone will always buy you a drink"

Chris Isaacs is 46 and used to work as a driver, but he has now been unemployed for a year. He is divorced and lives with his sister and mother in Retreat, a colored township outside Cape Town.

I was born in De Aar, up country. I left school at 13 and got a job as a gas pump attendant until I moved to Cape Town. Since than I've had a series of jobs, driving both trucks and cars for Thomas Cook, Rent-a-Truck, and the British Consulate. I worked at the consulate for eleven

Chris has to live with his mother in her small bungalow.

months. You have to be careful in a job like that because you hear some interesting things while you are driving.

Then I fell ill and had to leave. It's difficult to get another job. You have to have references, a "book of life" (identity card), and an unemployment card. Without those, you can't get anything. I've got good references but it's still difficult, so I've stopped looking for a job.

Retreat, near Cape Town, where unemployment affects almost every family in the township.

The people at the labor bureau don't help much. If they offer you a job, you have to take it, even if it is not your kind of work. You don't have a choice because if you refuse, they won't give you any money. I've just applied for a disability allowance. I had been putting it off because I didn't want to live on charity, and it's only ninety-three rand a month. If I then earn more than twenty rand a month, they will take it away again.

I got divorced in 1981. My ex-wife works as a domestic servant and our three children live with her. I ought to be paying them some money, but at the moment, they know I can't. I live with my mother, who lives on a pension, and my sister, a factory supervisor, and they support me. I make us a bit of extra money by transporting liquor for the local *shebeen*.

You can't sell alcohol without a license in South Africa. It's difficult and expensive to get one and the laws on drink are very strict. However, there are people who run illegal bars, or *shebeens*. They are quite common in the poorer areas of town. The police know about them but they are difficult to control, and if they were closed down, others would spring up in their place. Most of the time the police turn a blind eye. Then, every three months or so, they make a raid and confiscate the alcohol, but once the police have gone, it's business as usual.

The *shebeen* is the only place I can afford to go. You can spend all day there and talk to your friends. Everyone drinks Virginia, which is a very cheap white wine. If you don't have any money, someone will always offer to buy you a drink, and you can usually get a week's credit. Without the *shebeens*, I couldn't afford to go out at all.

"We have 7,000 species of plants here"

Christine Malan is 41 and is a botanist at the Kirstenbosch National Botanic Gardens, on the side of Table Mountain, near Cape Town. She lives with her husband and 14-year-old son in a cottage in the gardens.

The Ice Age affected Africa as well as Europe and North America, and one of its results was that plants were forced southward until they reached the Cape, where they had to find a niche. South Africa now has the richest variety of plant life in the world and we have about 7,000 different species of plants here at Kirstenbosch, including about 1,400 endangered ones. A large number of Europe's most commonly cultivated plants, such as geraniums and gladioli, originally came from South Africa.

The climate has been largely responsible for this great variety of plant life. It is very complex, but basically, inland they have hot summers and cold, frosty winters. The eastern Transvaal and Natal have a subtropical climate with hot, humid, and wet summers. The Cape has a Mediterranean climate and gets its rain in the winter. It has the best farming conditions in South Africa. The rainfall decreases as you go from east to west, but the average temperature tends to be much the same throughout the country. This is because differences in latitude are compensated for by the fact that the inland, northern areas are much higher.

Christine's main aim is to get the young visitors interested in plants.

The varied climate results in many varied types of vegetation. We have desert and semi-desert, veld, temperate grassland, forest, and "Mediterranean" plants and shrubs. It is in the last of these that we specialize at Kirstenbosch. We have a wide range of evergreen shrubs which have adapted to withstand the summer drought, such as erica and protea. The giant protea is South Africa's national flower, but altogether we have eighty-two species of protea at Kirstenbosch.

Although I trained as a botanist, my main function here involves education. People tend to think that botany is the concern of scientists and has nothing to do with them. Therefore one of our main aims at Kirstenbosch is to change people's attitudes toward plants and to increase their awareness and appreciation. We get 400,000 visitors a year, so it's a big job. One of my duties is to look after the 17,000 schoolchildren who come here every year. I arrange guides for them and confer with the teachers to set up suitable educational programs. It's important to get the children involved by giving them worksheets, special projects, and competitions. We also get them to weed and replant areas of veld for us, which is something they never forget. I really enjoy working with the children because they seem to appreciate and care about nature more than adults do.

The giant protea, South Africa's national flower.

"Some day I'll have to go to Mecca"

Tayeb Rossier is a 64-year-old Malay, who has been working freelance as an architectural restorer for the last twenty years. He has recently been asked by the government to help set up a Malay workshop that will restore many of Cape Town's finest buildings.

When the Dutch arrived in the Cape in the seventeenth century, there were very few skilled craftsmen, so they brought in forty Malays, a race well known for their

Today Cape Town is a thriving, modern city, but Tayeb wants to save its past.

workmanship. There are now 150,000 Malays in South Africa, most of them living in the Cape Peninsula.

There is an old Malay quarter in the center of Cape Town, which is gradually being restored, but most Malays used to live in another district, now known as Dis-

trict 6. It was a very picturesque area and if the government had cared as much about restoration ten years ago as it does now, I think that District 6 would still exist. However, it occupied a very central position in the city, which was considered to be prime redevelopment land. So the people were moved out and a bulldozer was moved in to destroy everything except the churches and mosques.

Things do change, however. The government is currently setting up a project to restore old buildings, many of which show the original skill of Malay craftsmen. It is a continuation of our tradition that Malay workers are now restoring these buildings.

My job involves copying and restoring existing moldings, but sometimes I have to work just from architectural drawings. When this happens, my first step is to make a model out of clay, which is easier to work with than other materials. I then make a mold out of plaster of paris or rubber. Finally I cast the piece that I want, either in plaster of paris or cement. I use sisal to strengthen the mold. I am currently making moldings for Bertram House, a beautiful late Georgian town house in Cape Town.

I am one of a large family, with seven brothers and three sisters, but I never married because I've always liked to be free to travel. One day I will have to go to Mecca, the center of the Muslim faith. Religion is very important in our community, and we still faithfully carry out feasts, weddings, and pilgrimages according to our faith. In South Africa today, you will still see a Muslim wearing a fez, and *chalifah*, a traditional display of sword-

dancing, is still performed.

Malays don't like their children to go to Christian schools because they feel the Muslim faith is the most important part of their children's education. I left school at 11 and went to work for an architectural restoration firm. They helped me in my training, but much of the time I had to struggle along on my own as I wasn't allowed to go to the art classes. Things are changing now but it's a slow process and there's a long way to go.

A good deal of Cape Town's finest architecture owes its survival to Malay craftsmen.

"I've never had a vacation"

Saroj Govinsamy runs her mother's stall in the Indian Market in Durban. She is 26 and lives with her husband and his family. Although her family has been in South Africa since about 1820, they still maintain Indian traditions and customs.

There are about 800,000 Indians in South Africa and most of them live in Natal. They came in the nineteenth century to work on the sugar plantations and most of them stayed here. Some are Hindus, others are Muslims, and there are various different types of each, all speaking different languages. Because of this, many Indians use English as their main language. I am a Tamil Hindu and I have a red spot on my forehead to show it. I wear a yellow string around my neck as a sign that I am married.

I got married at 18. Although many marriages in the Indian community are still arranged by the parents, I met Patrick, my husband, by chance. My mother liked him so there was no problem about getting married. Among Indians, a woman must take her husband's religion and because Patrick is a Roman Catholic, we had a Roman Catholic wedding. I respect both Hinduism and Roman Catholicism. I live with Patrick, his parents, and our youngest daughter, who is 2. I have another daughter who is 7, but at the

Saroj sells everything from fruit to pictures of Indian gods, at her stall.

moment she is living with my mother.

My father bought this stall thirty years ago when the market first opened. I left school when I was 12, so that I could help him out, and I have been working here full time since he died twelve years ago. I have what is called a general dealer's license, which means I can sell only certain items. Even so, I am lucky to have a license at all, as they are very difficult to get. I sell a lot of incense, holy pictures, betel nut, and betel leaf. Betel nuts are grown in the Far East on a kind of palm tree. The nut is mixed with a little lime juice and then it is wrapped in betel leaf, ready for chewing. You can always tell if a man chews betel nut, because his mouth will be stained red by the juice. They are very popular among Asians and it is said one-tenth of the world's population chews betel nuts.

I buy my goods from a wholesaler who imports them from India. He comes to the market to take orders and to make deliveries. I have to pay fifty-six rand a month plus sales tax for the stall. In the end, I make about fifty rand a week profit if I'm lucky.

I never have any time to myself so I don't have any hobbies. I work here six days a week, from 6 a.m. until 2 p.m. When I get home I have to cook, do the washing, and then prepare for the next day. I've never had a vacation. I only stop working on Sundays and public holidays. My only other rest comes when my younger brother has a school vacation and can take over for a while. My brother has stayed at school longer than I did because Indians consider it more important for a son to gain a good education than a daughter. The son must become the main breadwinner of the family and it is thought that a good education will help him to succeed. My brother's education will benefit us all because if he does well, his family will share in his success.

There are hundreds of stalls in the market. Saroj's is number 569.

"We brew beer and have lots of parties"

Joyce Mfeka, 51, is a Zulu and was born in a village on the south coast of Natal. Since the death of her husband, she has worked as a housemaid in Durban. She lives in a room at the back of the apartment where she works.

My father used to cut sugarcane before he died and my mother, who is still alive, was a housewife. I left school at 13, because my father wanted me to get married, but in the end, I helped in the house and on the farm for three years and didn't marry until I was 16. I was brought up as a Catholic and met my husband in church. He was a train mechanic. He gave my father ten cows as the *lobola* and my father then gave them to my brother so that he in turn could pay for a wife.

I have four children between 16 and 24 years old. They all work except for my youngest daughter, who's on my mother's farm and is waiting to get married. My husband died of a heart attack long ago. I got some money from his company every month for three years after his death, so that at first I didn't need to work. Then, at the age of 31, I had to find my first job.

I've worked as a housemaid for twenty years now. I've always lived with the family for whom I've been working. My own children also lived with me. I've had a boyfriend, Philip, for the last 15 years and he has been living with me too. He's a

Joyce does all the housework for the girls she works for.

decorator and works for himself.

Now I work for two girls who have an apartment in Berea, which is an old area of Durban. I do the housework, wash and iron the clothes, and wash the dishes and their cars.

I live in a *kia*, which is a room out at the back of the apartment with its own toilet. It faces a lane which runs along the backs of all the houses. Some *kias* have electricity, but mine doesn't so I have to use candles for light.

Most maids live in *kias*, although some of them commute from their own homes to work everyday. I know all the maids around here and have a lot of friends to enjoy myself with. We brew beer and have lots of parties.

Last year, the girls who own the apartment took me to the beach. It was the first time that I'd ever been there. The water didn't stand still and I was frightened. Zulus use salt water to prevent illness, but they never go to the beach for fun.

My children sometimes come to see me and sometimes I go to see my mother, who still lives on the farm. It's only about 70 kilometers (45 miles) away, but it takes me about three and a half hours to get there by bus. I was given thirteen cows for my two daughters when they married and the cows are kept on the farm. When my mother dies the land will go my brother, but when he dies it will go to my children before his children because I am the first-born. But it doesn't matter who owns the land because we all look after each other. When I get too old to work I know that I will be well looked after.

The white building is Joyce's kia, *which has running water, but no electricity.*

"We had to build the church ourselves"

Dr Piet Meiring is 43 and a minister of the Dutch Reformed Church at Lynnwood Ridge, in Pretoria. Before taking up his current position, he was a minister at a hospital and then a professor of theology.

There have been ministers in my family for more than 200 years. The first was a Dutchman who, on his way to Indonesia in 1743, was persuaded to settle in the Cape. I was born in Johannesburg and grew up in a parsonage as my father was a minister. I took my degree at the university here in Pretoria and obtained my doctorate at the Free University of Amsterdam in the Netherlands.

As a minister, I have worked in three different fields and each one has been an enjoyable experience in its own way. My first assignment was as minister of a hospital at Riviera in Pretoria. The job was very demanding because there were a lot of young nurses and medical students in the congregation who were being exposed to the realities of death and suffering for the first time. I was then offered the post of Professor of Theology at the Black University of the North, near Pietersburg. It gave me a great opportunity to get to know black students, and their hopes and grievances.

In 1975, I was called to a new congregation at Lynnwood Ridge in Pretoria. When I arrived there was not much in the way of facilities and money, so we had to build

Piet talks to children in the church built by the congregation and himself.

Piet came to understand the feelings of Blacks during his time at Pietersburg.

the church ourselves. It has been the most rewarding job I've ever had although we have had our problems. It took much discussion before we decided to be a church that was open to all, but I think we made the right decision.

A very high proportion of Whites, Blacks, and Coloreds belong to one Christian Church or another. Some, like the Anglicans and the Roman Catholics, are more racially integrated in their worship and organization than others, such as the Dutch Reformed Church, which has different senates for different racial groups. Some ministers say the Church should remain apart from politics, but others feel that it should address social problems.

The Dutch Reformed Church is currently going through an identity crisis.

The ideals and aspirations of the Afrikaans people and their Church have often been identical and the Church has been uncritical in its support of government policies. That hasn't always been a good thing. For example, apartheid was given a theological justification by the Church, without due consideration of the issues involved. You can't just use the Bible to suit your own purposes. There is a struggle in the Church between those who want to maintain the status quo and those who say we should be taking a more prophetic stance. In other words, we can either mirror society in all aspects, both good and bad, or we can attempt to create a better life for everyone. There are so many walls, cliffs, and rivers dividing people here. The Church should try to break down these barriers. It should be working for reconciliation and helping all people to live together in harmony.

Facts

Capital city: Pretoria (population 750,000).

Language: South Africa has two official languages: English and Afrikaans. There are also eight officially recognized Bantu languages: Northern, Western, and Southern Sotho, Zulu, Swazi, Xhosa, Venda, and Tsonga.

Currency: The rand was introduced in 1961, replacing the South African pound. There are 100 cents to the rand. $1.00 U.S. = 2 rand.

Population: 31,010,000 (1982 estimate), about a quarter of whom live in the southern Transvaal conurbation centered on Johannesburg. The South African population is growing at a rate of about 2.5 percent a year. Transvaal has 11 million inhabitants, Cape Province 6 million, Natal 3.5 million, and the Orange Free State 2.5 million. 8 million people live in the black homelands within South Africa's borders. The four major cities are Johannesburg (with 2 million inhabitants), Cape Town (with 1.5 million), Durban, and Pretoria. Among all races, there has been a marked drift of the rural population into the cities. Many of the black townships such as Soweto are growing very quickly and have large estimated populations.

Race: About 68 percent of South Africans are black, 16 percent white, 12 percent of colored, or mixed, descent, and 4 percent of Asian stock.

Climate: The climate varies from region to region. The coastal regions of Cape province are temperate, with rain in winter, Natal and the eastern Transvaal are subtropical, with wet and humid summers, and the interior plateau has hot summers, cold winters, and a low rainfall.

Religion: Christian churches, including many Bantu ones, account for about three-quarters of the population. The largest of these is the Dutch Reformed Church, to which over half of the Whites belong. There are significant numbers of Hindus and Muslims.

Government: South Africa left the British Commonwealth and became a republic in 1961. Pretoria is the administrative capital and Cape Town the legislative capital. The country is divided into four provinces, which administer many local services, and there are ten self-governing black homelands, six of which have been declared independent republics. The new constitution of 1984 divides the South African Parliament into three chambers: the House of Assembly for Whites, the House of Representatives for Coloreds, and the House of Deputies for Indians. The president is elected by a committee drawn from the three houses. Blacks are unrepresented and their affairs are controlled by the Department of Bantu Administration and Development.

Housing: Public housing is racially segregated and each race is confined to living in designated areas. Housing is poor in the black townships and there is a severe shortage for Coloreds and Indians.

Education: Elementary and secondary schools fall under provincial administration, but the education of Blacks and Coloreds is administered separately. Education is compulsory for Whites and Coloreds, but for Blacks it is neither compulsory nor free. Consequently, only one-tenth of black children enter secondary school. There are sixteen universities, which are also racially segregated, and a wide variety of technical colleges.

Agriculture: Livestock is reared in large numbers, and there are valuable wine, fruit, fishing, and cotton industries. South Africa is self-sufficient in food supplies. The agricultural sector is still the biggest employer in the country, with about 3 million people working on the land, and it accounts for 7 percent of the gross domestic product.

Industry: Mining is a vital area of industry for South Africa. The export of gold, diamonds, and uranium is one of the country's greatest sources of wealth. Manufacturing industry is expanding rapidly and accounts for a quarter of the gross domestic product. Development is dependent on the white population's capital and expertise, and on the unskilled labor of the other races. The wage gap between Whites and Blacks (most of whom are not allowed to join trade unions) remains a source of discontent. It is estimated that in the mining industry the average wage of Whites is twelve times that of Blacks, and four times that of Asians.

he Media: The Press is vigorous and some sectors **f** it oppose government policies. English language **e**wspapers have considerable freedom of expres**s**on. In all, there are eight Afrikaans and fourteen **E**nglish dailies, but there is a monopoly over a **l**rge area of the Press. Government and commer**c**ial radio stations reach most of the population, **b**ut there is only one television channel in South **A**frica. It broadcasts programs in English and Afri**k**aans. A second channel, broadcasting in five **B**antu languages, is soon to be opened.

Acknowledgments

The cover photograph and those on pages 6, **,** 29, 35 (right), 37 (right), 49, and 50 were **s**upplied by the South African Tourist Corpo**r**ation

Glossary

Acacia   A small, thorny tree with yellow or white flowers.

Afrikaans   The language, based on Dutch, developed by the seventeenth- and eighteenth-century Dutch settlers.

Apartheid   The official South African policy of racial segregation, which results in different laws and living conditions for different races.

Artifact   Any instrument or tool developed by cultures of the past.

Bantu   The black peoples who inhabit southern Africa; also their language.

Bushmen   The nomadic hunters and gatherers who live in the Kalahari Desert.

Coloreds   The official South African term for people descended from mixed marriages between Whites and Hottentots, Bushmen, or Blacks.

Cull   To reduce the numbers in a herd by killing the weakest animals.

Doctorate   The highest possible qualification in any field.

Fanakalo   A language developed for communication in South Africa's gold mines.

Hindu   A person believing in Hinduism, the main religion of India.

Homeland   A self-governing area for Blacks within South Africa. Six of these homelands are termed independent republics, but they are not internationally recognized.

Impala   A southern African antelope famous for its ability to take huge leaps.

Kraal   A small group of huts which is often home for just one family.

Lobola   The payment made by a bridegroom to the bride's father before a marriage takes place. The custom is widespread among South African Blacks.

Mute   Unable to communicate by sound.

Spanner   A wrench, or monkey wrench.

Springbok   A species of antelope common in South Africa.

Township   A town built especially for non-Whites. Townships are often found just outside the major cities.

Veld   An area of open grassland on high ground.

Index